A Journey Down th

Written and illustrated by
Scoular Anderson

Richard Drew Publishing, Glasgow

✲✥✲✥✲✥✲✥✲✥✲✥✲✥✲✥✲✥✲✥✲✥✲✥✲✥✲✥✲✥✲
For my sister
✲✥✲✥✲✥✲✥✲✥✲✥✲✥✲✥✲✥✲✥✲✥✲✥✲✥✲✥✲✥✲

British Library Cataloguing in Publication Data
Anderson, Scoular
  A journey down the Clyde.
  1. Scotland. Strathclyde Region. Clyde River, history
  I. Title
  941.4′1
  ISBN 0-86267-266-X

First published 1990 by Richard Drew Publishing Ltd,
6 Clairmont Gardens, Glasgow G3 7LW Scotland

Copyright © 1990 Scoular Anderson

Designed by James W. Murray
Printed and bound in Great Britain

FOR thousands of years people have lived, worked and played beside the River Clyde. Its name means 'sheltered spot'.

It's not possible to sail all the way down the river in a boat but in a book we can imagine the journey and look out for the signs left by people who lived by the river. Some are ancient, others are more recent.

Let's make the trip!

The Clyde begins its journey in the Lowther Hills in Southern Scotland. Lead was mined here in Roman times and the remains of Roman roads can still be seen. Later, the Kings of Scotland called the area 'God's treasure house in Scotland' because of the gold that was found here. Today the main road and rail routes from England run alongside the river at this point.

THE river flows on. At Abington there are the remains of a 12th century fort (left). It is known as a motte and bailey. The motte is the mound of earth which would have had a wooden tower on top. A wooden wall (the bailey) protected one side of the fort while the Clyde protected the other.

The Clyde makes its way round Tinto Hill, the tallest hill in the area (right). It's sometimes known as Tintock Tap. At the summit there is a huge Bronze Age cairn.

At the foot of Tinto, near Fallburn, there is another Bronze Age site — the remains of a fort. The protective ditches and ramparts can easily be seen among the heather (bottom right).

The river flows towards Biggar then away again. The break in the hills here is known as the Biggar Gap (below). It is thought the Clyde once flowed through here a long time ago. It joined the River Tweed to travel east rather than west as it does today.

THE river now passes the village of New Lanark which was founded in 1784. Two men, Arkwright (an expert on cotton-spinning) and Dale (who provided money) harnessed the waters of the Clyde to power their cotton mills. At one time they were the biggest cotton mills in Britain. Another partner in the enterprise, David Owen, added housing and a school.

Today the Clyde is used for power by the Electricity Board and it controls the flow of water over the Falls of Clyde. The Falls are called the Stoneybyres Falls, the Corra Linn and Bonnington Linn.

150 years ago, a famous artist William Turner painted the Bonnington Linn where the river passes through a narrow, rocky gorge.

Near Lanark a man releases his racing pigeons. These are young birds in training and he stops to let them go every morning on his way to work.

THE river now meanders through a pleasant valley called Clydesdale. The area is famous for its fruit-growing. As long ago as the eighth century it was known as the 'appleyards of Lanark'. Some nurseries specialize in vegetables like leeks or 'scotch' tomatoes. In others you can pick your own raspberries or strawberries and there are many garden centres selling flowers and shrubs.

Clydesdale horses were first bred here in the 18th century. They were used for heavy farm work and transporting coal.

The river wanders on between gentle tree-lined banks, past the ruins of Cambusnethan House. This is a favourite part of the river for fishermen.

THE towns of Hamilton and Motherwell sit on hills on either side of the Clyde. Here the river has been diverted so that an artificial loch could be made.

It's called Strathclyde Loch and is used for recreations like sailing, board-sailing and canoeing. You can jog round the shores of the loch or just sit and have a picnic.

At the south end of the loch its waters drain into the Clyde over a man-made waterfall.

On the other side of the river stands the Hamilton Mausoleum. It was built by the 10th Duke of Hamilton to commemorate his family. Their castle, which stood nearby, had to be demolished because it was in danger of collapsing into a coal mine!

NOW the Clyde snakes its way between wooded slopes. Above one bend of the river the great red sandstone walls of Bothwell Castle tower above the trees. Although a ruin, the castle has had a long and colourful history and many owners.

It was built in the 13th century by the de Moravia family. It was demolished in the following century then rebuilt by Black Archibald the Grim, Earl of Douglas.

In some places the walls are four and a half metres thick. The great tower or donjon (left) had its own moat and drawbridge within the courtyard.

As the river nears Glasgow it passes Glasgow Green. This was once the centre of city life. It was used for grazing the town's cattle and sheep — and for drying clothes. The monument rising above the trees (left) was the first one in the country to be raised to Admiral Lord Nelson. There are two unusual buildings on the Green. One used to house Templeton's Carpet Factory (right) and was built to resemble the Doge's Palace in Venice. Nearby you can still see the poles where Glaswegians hung up their washing lines.

The other building is the People's Palace (bottom left) which is a museum of Glasgow's history. It has a large glasshouse attached to it called the Winter Gardens where you can sit among exotic plants and have a snack. Rowing clubs hold races and regattas on this part of the river.

THE river-bank has perhaps changed more in the city than anywhere else. There are always new buildings going up and the sooty, smoky Victorian city has become a place of smart, clean stone, steel and glittering glass.

The St Enoch's shopping centre towers like a mountain range behind St Andrew's Cathedral.

THE river is crossed by about 50 bridges along its length. The first bridge in Glasgow (a wooden one) was built 800 years ago. It no longer stands but there are plenty of others like the busy Kingston motorway bridge or the Central Station railway bridge (above). Bell's Bridge was built for the Garden Festival in 1988.

There are tunnels too. The modern Clyde tunnel is for vehicles but you can still see the round towers on the banks of the river which were entrances to a much older tunnel used by pedestrians and horses and carts.

Sometimes the Clyde was so busy in Glasgow that you could cross the river by stepping from one boat to another — or so the story goes! It's a quieter river now. The disused warehouses have been pulled down and the quays turned into walkways. The bollards where the ships tied up are the only reminder of the past.

A riverside mosque brings a touch of eastern architecture to the city. Across the river the old fish market no longer sells fish. It has been done up to sell other things (bottom).

The giant Finnieston Crane has been preserved as a monument to the great industries of the Clyde. It was used to load steam engines on to ships bound for all corners of the world. A glass-covered hotel now stands where ships once unloaded their cargo.

THE banks of the river at Glasgow and Clydebank have been used for ship-building for a long time. Many great and famous ships have been launched into the narrow Clyde. Today, only a handful of these yards remain, like Govan (above).

Some of the city's docks have been filled in. Each dock specialised in a certain type of cargo — wood or livestock or perhaps general goods. Grain was landed at Meadowside Quay and stored in the huge granary (top). Rothesay Dock handled coal and ores.

A new machine stands where there were once warehouses. It's like a giant waste-disposal unit, gobbling up chunks of metal, even cars, and breaking them into small pieces for recycling.

LEAVING Glasgow behind the Clyde flows under Erskine Bridge which is a type called a cable stayed girder bridge and carries traffic high above the river.

Just beyond is Bowling Harbour. A canal starts here and crosses Scotland. It was built in the 18th century to link the River Clyde with the River Forth. Although most of the canal cannot be used now, the lock-gates and the customs house can be seen at Bowling. There is also a railway swing bridge and just behind, a smaller bascule bridge which tipped up to let ships pass through.

The Erskine ferry is the only remaining passenger ferry crossing the upper part of the Clyde.

BETWEEN Bowling and Dumbarton the river was once so shallow that you could wade across at low tide. Many plans were made to deepen the river for shipping. In the 18th century an underwater wall was built to control the water. It was called the 'Lang Dyke' and it still stands, marked by towers and buoys.

At Dumbarton there is a spectacular landmark — a giant lump of volcanic rock on the banks of the river. There have been fortifications on it since ancient times. Mary Queen of Scots visited the castle in 1548 and the present castle dates mostly from the 17th century.

The 'Waverley' is the last sea-going paddle-steamer in the world and makes regular sailings down the river in summer.

Flocks of birds feed on the mudflats here. They are just a few of the many birds that live near the river, from moorhens on the upper reaches to eider ducks on the Firth. Other birds you are likely to see are cormorants, oyster-catchers, curlews and shelducks.

Downriver from Dumbarton the Clyde becomes deeper. In the 17th century some Glasgow merchants raised money to build a harbour on the coast here. (At this time, ships couldn't sail all the way to Glasgow.) The harbour became known as New Port Glasgow then just Port Glasgow.

Newark Castle is a smart, fortified mansion at Port Glasgow. When it was built in the 15th and 16th centuries it stood alone by the Clyde but now it is surrounded by shipyards. The owners of the castle used to keep pigeons in the beehive shaped doocot.

The town of Port Glasgow became well-known for ship-building, rope-making and sail-making. The old Port Glasgow Ropeworks building still stands.

The 'Comet' was one of the first steam-ships in the world to operate a passenger ferry service. It was built at Port Glasgow and sailed on this part of the Clyde. A replica of the ship sits in Port Glasgow town centre.

These gravestones are at Kilmun. On churchyard stones you will see how many people made their living from the river — as ship-builders, sailors or fishermen.

THE port of Greenock was once famous for its herring-fishery and its shipbuilding. It has a grand customs house facing the river. In front of the building is a very ornate lamp known as the Beacon Fountain. Above the customs house door is a coat of arms with a very jolly unicorn and a rather sad lion.

In Victoria Harbour the tugs and pilot boats wait to help ships navigate the river.

This is also the berth of the 'Torch', the ship which goes out to refuel the buoys with gas for their lights. There are about 180 navigation lights on the river. The buoys are regularly brought back to the depot to have seaweed and barnacles scraped off.

BEYOND Greenock the river broadens and becomes the Firth of Clyde. The area of water just off Greenock and Gourock is known as the 'Tail o' the Bank'. Great liners and cargo ships used to anchor here and wait for high tide to take them up river.

Today it is the smaller boats that use the Firth. There are pleasure steamers, coast guards and police launches. There are submarines from the British and American naval bases.

There are car-ferries plying between Gourock and Dunoon, Hunter's Quay, Wemyss Bay, Rothesay, Ardrossan and Brodick. There are coasters, yachts, speed-boats and fishing-boats.

There are 'hoppers' dumping sand and mud from the dredger 'Blytheswood'. There is only one dredger left on the river, keeping it deep enough for shipping.

TOWARDS the end of the last century the coasts of the Firth of Clyde became popular for holidays. The easiest way to reach these places was by boat so many piers were built for the passengers — there were 65 at one time. Some piers were decorative, like Dunoon with its Chinese pagoda. Most, like Kirn, have fallen into disuse and become roosts for sea-birds.

Cargo was carried by boat, too. In some of the harbours like Millport (left) and Rothesay (right) you can see the public weigh-bridges where cargo was weighed once it was loaded on to a cart or lorry.

ONCE piers had been built then houses quickly followed. Holiday villas, cottages and hotels sprang up. The Victorians built their houses in all shapes and sizes. A castle design, like this house at Cove, was a favourite idea.

In 1902 the architect Charles Rennie Mackintosh was asked to design a house for the publisher Walter Blackie. The house was built at Helensburgh and looks a bit castle-like too.

In the sitting-room there is a little drawer specially designed to hold a telescope. Walter Blackie liked to watch the ships pass on the Clyde.

Once the houses were built they were often ornately decorated.

Perhaps carved wooden barge-boarding was added to the end of a roof, like this one in Rothesay.

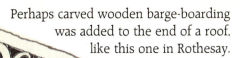

... or gateposts like shells at Cove.

... or a 'chucky-stane gate' of white quartz stones at Blairmore ...

... or a decorative porch ...

and of course, lots of windows facing the sea. ...

ALTHOUGH people prefer to take holidays abroad nowadays, there are still plenty of holidaymakers and day-trippers at the Clyde Coast. You will find them sunbathing (sometimes) at Rothesay, buying ice-cream at Brodick or going fishing from Largs to catch mackerel and cod. Then there are post cards to post. The Post Office at Hunter's Quay is 100 years old. It was built specially to serve the yacht owners who gathered to race there.

SOME yachts are lifted into sheds for the winter but many stay in the water all year round. Several marinas on the Clyde have berths for hundreds of boats.

At Largs you can fuel your boat at the Clyde's first maritime filling station (left).

There are signs of past days of sea-faring scattered here and there — like a collection of old anchors at Port Bannatyne (below). 'Puffers' were once a common sight. These little ships transported coal and other goods around the Clyde and the Western Isles. A puffer can be seen at the Scottish Maritime Museum at Irvine (right) along with other river craft. Irvine used to be one of Glasgow's ports.

There are industrial landmarks here too. There is an oil-fired power-station at Inverkip and a nuclear one at Hunterston. Between the two are the giant cranes of the Hunterston Deep Water Terminal where large ships can unload cargo, mostly iron-ore.

WHEN it grows dark over the river the navigation lights begin to wink their warning to ships of rocks and shallows. The first light-house on the Clyde was built on the highest point of the Island of Little Cumbrae in the middle of the Firth. It was constructed in 1757 and a coal fire provided the light. It can be seen standing above the present light-house. Other familiar landmarks are (from the left) The Cloch, Toward Point, Ardrossan Harbour, The Gantock and Turnberry.

NOW the Firth of Clyde is broad and windswept. The sea dashes against the 60 metre-high sandstone cliffs at the Heads of Ayr or rolls on to the long sandy beaches at Irvine and Troon. The grassy lands beside these beaches are known as links. They are an ideal place for golf-courses and there are famous golf-links at Troon (below) and Turnberry.

Little fishermen's cottages snuggle round the harbour at Dunure while the castle of Culzean stands proudly on its cliff-top. The architect Robert Adam built this grand house for the 10th Earl of Cassilis in the 18th century. An older castle stood on the same site.

AILSA Craig is a large cone of volcanic rock which stands alone in the middle of the Firth. It's also known as 'Paddy's Milestone' because it's halfway between Glasgow and Ireland.

Colonies of seabirds live here, like the gannets which plummet into the water from a great height to catch fish. The hard granite of Ailsa Craig was used to make excellent curling stones.

And somewhere between Ailsa Craig and Pladda Island off Arran, the River Clyde becomes the sea. . . .